Saint Bernadette Speaks - Book 1

Published by Abba Books LLC
abbabooksllc@gmail.com
Copyright © 2023 Marie-Josée Thibault

All Rights Reserved

No part of this publication may be reproduced, distributed, or transmitted in any form or by any means, including photocopying, recording, or other electronic or mechanical methods, without the prior written permission of the publisher.

First Edition, 2023
Designed and Edited by Abba Books LLC
ISBN: 979-8-9875984-8-1

Abba Books LLC
34972 Newark Blvd, #441
Newark, CA 94560

www.abbamyfatheriloveyou.com
https://www.facebook.com/AbbaILoveYouBooks/

Contents

Preface	VI
Chapt 1	1
Chapt 2	5
Chapt 3	7
Chapt 4	9
Chapt 5	10
Chapt 6	15
Chapt 7	17
Chapt 8	19
Chapt 9	21
Chapt 10	25
Chapt 11	29
Chapt 12	31
Chapt 13	35
Chapt 14	41
Chapt 15	43
Chapt 16	45
Chapt 17	47
Chapt 18	53
Chapt 19	55
Chapt 20	57
Chapt 21	59
Chapt 22	61
Chapt 23	63
Chapt 24	65
Chapt 25	67
Chapt 26	71
Chapt 27	75
Chapt 28	77
Chapt 29	81
Chapt 30	85
Chapt 31	87
Chapt 32	89
Chapt 33	91
Chapt 34	93
Chapt 35	95
Afterword	97
About the Author	98
Also by Author	99

Preface

Dear Children of the Earth,

It is such a delight to bring the words of Saint Bernadette to you! Whenever I see her walk into my living room once a week for a dictation, I am always amazed by her vibrant youth, gracious demeanor, and ceaseless, genuine smile. With the Curé Peyramale always at her side, she lifts me up emotionally and spiritually, and she solves all my silly problems in an instant. I love her so much!

Rejoice in the words of hope and clarity about the mysteries of the powerful grotto of Lourdes, all taught by Bernadette herself.

Bernadette, I love you!

Marie-Josée

FREE DOWNLOAD

Get your free copy of :
"Saint Padre Pio Speaks: Book 1"
when you sign up to the
author's VIP mailing list!
Get started here:

www.abbamyfatheriloveyou.com

Saint Bernadette Speaks

1

My children, my dear friends of the earth, I am Saint Bernadette, born Bernadette Soubirous.

I am delighted to speak with you today for I have prayed for this blessed moment between us for a long time. The Eternal Father has finally agreed, and I am here now—even though in fact I have never left you.

Saint Bernadette Speaks

Verily, verily I say unto you, the Most Blessed Virgin Mary loves you, Jesus Christ our Savior and our God loves you, the Living and Almighty Father loves you, the Benevolent Holy Spirit loves you, and I love you as well, much more than written words can express.

The expression of our love for you is experienced in your heart, dear little beloved soul, through the miracles of Heaven brought to you every day, regardless of your perception of these same miracles.

My mission on earth, which began in Lourdes, which continued after my death, which is magnified day by day, and which still continues, forever and ever, is to teach you the grace of miracles, by virtue of my gift of miracles and the miraculous Lourdes water.

Alleluia! Alleluia! Alleluia! Blessed are those who believe with unwavering faith without seeing, for they shall inherit eternal life. Amen. Alleluia!

Saint *Bernadette* Speaks

2   My children, I am so happy to finally be able to speak to you! Thousands and thousands of pilgrims visit the Sanctuary of Lourdes at any given time, and therefore, my desire to talk to each and everyone is so great!

I am infinitely grateful to Marie-Josée, the essence of Saint Paul on earth, who is taking this dictation at this very moment. Above all, I am infinitely grateful to God, our Father Almighty, Who has accepted my requests and prayers in favor of the diffusion of my message on earth at this point in the history of humanity.

My message is this: the miracles taking place in Lourdes and everywhere on earth are readily available and accessible to all! I will teach you the grace of miracles and it will be granted to you by God the Father Almighty Himself.

Alleluia! Alleluia! Alleluia! Blessed are those invited to Lourdes, the fountain of miracles in your heart. Amen. Alleluia!

Saint *Bernadette* Speaks

3   My beloved children of the earth, I am here in Paradise, at the moment you are reading these lines. Here in Paradise, where I live with the other Saints you know, the pure Souls, the Angels of God, the Most Blessed Virgin Mary, the Holy Spirit, Christ Jesus our Savior and our God, and God the Eternal Father, the beatitudes of the Great Beyond are perpetual and inefabble. Come join us after the passage that is death! I pray for your soul, for its redemption in the Light of Christ, Who is the very Hope of the Kingdom. Amen. Alleluia!

Alleluia! Alleluia! Alleluia! Blessed is he who believes in Christ the Savior, our Lord and our God, for this one will inherit eternal life in Heaven with us! Amen. Alleluia!

Saint Bernadette Speaks

4   My children, it is my great pleasure to speak to you about Lourdes in France. Lourdes, my Holy Sanctuary, is a small part of the world that contains within its physical plane an extraordinary and mystical energy seen nowhere else on planet earth. In fact, the holy and blessed water flowing near the Grotto of Our Lady of Lourdes comes to you directly from Paradise where its source is located. Do you see?

That is why the miracles taking place through the miraculous Lourdes water are so numerous, in fact, much more numerous than you can imagine. Indeed, hundreds of thousands of people around the world pray and are dedicated to Our Lady of Lourdes, our dear Mother Whom I met in 1858, and Her intercession before God is extraordinarily powerful and universal. For Our Lady of Lourdes encompasses the whole earth with Her miraculous and redemptive Powers, far beyond Lourdes. Amen. Alleluia!

When the Virgin Mary, the Immaculate Conception, appeared to me at the age of 14 years, I was in a very favorable inner spiritual state. Indeed, no one knew that, in fact, I prayed a lot, even at my young age, and I said my rosary every day. My faith was pure and personal and I had already developed an intimate and sincere relationship with the Virgin Mary. When the Virgin Mary appeared to me like this, this mystical vision was truly a sweet confirmation of my faith in her and a wonderful consolation offered by God.

When She asked me to fetch water under the earth that was there, I believed immediately the sacred words She had told me and my faith was unwavering. The eyes of my heart could see the miraculous water that sprang from the earth before my physical eyes could have seen. I was not confused because I was patient and spiritually supported by the Virgin Mary. When the miraculous spilled forth on its own in a small stream and was collected by the faithfuls who were present, my joy was unparalleled. The first miracles performed through the miraculous Lourdes water filled me with a mystical power and a peace of mind that I never knew could exist.

The Virgin Mary supported me, guided me, and instructed me in all the stages of my life that followed the discovery of the miraculous Lourdes water.

Alleluia! Alleluia! Alleluia! Blessed is the Virgin Mary, the Immaculate Conception, ineffable Power from Heaven on earth. Amen. Alleluia!

Saint *Bernadette* Speaks

6   My children, I am in Paradise now and I am watching you at this very moment you are reading these lines. Be strong and be fortified in your faith by virtue of these divine treasures that are given to you right now!

Heaven has opened for you, dear reader, dear little soul so sweet in my hands! Honor the blessing that God is giving you at this point in your life and thank Him! Say: "I give you thanks, O my God, O my Creator, for so much mercy in my life! Amen. Alleluia!"

Alleluia! Alleluia! Alleluia! Blessed is he who gives thanks to God every day of his life, for God in return blesses him. Amen. Alleluia!

Saint Bernadette Speaks

7   My children, I am pleased to speak to you today about the Most Blessed Virgin Mary.

When She appeared to me in 1858, at the age 14, I was in a state of mystical ecstasy. My age and my naiveté contributed favorably to my entry into this mystical ecstasy, due to the simplicity and the humility of my heart. Indeed, the Virgin Mary can not materialize herself to those who have not developed an advanced spiritual life, regardless of age. Moreover, the absence of fear is important to the success of any mystical experience.

Alleluia! Alleluia! Alleluia! Blessed are the simple and the humble of heart, for to those ones the Virgin Mary shall appear. Amen. Alleluia!

My children, I wish to speak to you today of Paradise existing in your heart. Yes my friend, my child, dear reader of this book blessed by God, the Kingdom of God promised by Christ, preeminent Emissary of the Father, is found nestled at the very depth of your heart; this is why we are capable of visiting you as we wish.

In addition, the miraculous Lourdes water, taking its source in Paradise, in fact, takes its source in your heart! Indeed, dear child, you carry the miraculous water in your heart and you can access it at any time you wish.

Saint Bernadette Speaks

8   The miraculous spring at Lourdes truly exists in Paradise. This miraculous spring is actually a beautiful little river running around small hills and undulations in Paradise. This miraculous river in Paradise, the very source of the miraculous Lourdes water, is visited constantly by us, the Saints in Paradise, the Angels of God, the Most Blessed Virgin Mary, the Holy Spirit, Jesus Christ our Savior and our God, under the benevolent Presence of the Merciful God. For it is He Who makes decisions with respect to each and every one of the miracles that are connected to the miraculous Lourdes water—and this, everywhere on earth.

Since you carry the Kingdom in your heart, dear friend, dear pilgrim, you carry consequently the miraculous divine river in your heart that is the source of the miraculous Lourdes water. Do you see? I will teach you very soon how to pray effectively for the obtention of miracles of your life by asking the intercession of the miraculous Lourdes water.

Alleluia! Alleluia! Alleluia! Blessed is he who believes my words, the words of Saint Bernadette, for God the Father will answer him. Amen. Alleluia!

My children, it is my sweet pleasure today to speak to you about the Virgin Mary.

The Virgin Mary, our Divine Mother to all, on earth as in Heaven, holds a mystical and universal Force unparalleled among the gifts of the Living God.

The Virgin Mary is much more than the Mother of Christ: She is the Mother of every soul that God the Father Almighty created.

Saint *Bernadette* Speaks

9   The Virgin Mary represents the Eternal Feminine Principle present in every form of life as created by God the Father Almighty. Moreover, the Virgin Mary was conceived and created at the time of Genesis, the cradle of the universe. Consequently, the Virgin Mary was born long before Mary of Nazareth, the physical mother of Jesus of Nazareth, walked the earth. The Virgin Mary, as explained here, is an ineffable Force of the entire universe, our Divine Mother to all, Who was created at the time of Genesis and Who lives in each and every one of your hearts, today, and world without end.

Alleluia! Alleluia! Alleluia! Blessed is the Virgin Mary, our Divine and Universal Mother to all. Amen. Alleluia!

Indeed, dear child, you carry the miraculous water in your heart and you can access it at any time you wish.

Saint *Bernadette* Speaks

10 My children, it is my pleasure today to speak to you about my life on earth as Bernadette Soubirous.

 I was born in a poor family, it is true, but my family was very religious and virtuous. My Father, though severe, was completely devoted to our family. My mother was pious, and despite her confusion and skepticism at the beginning of the apparitions, she believed in me and in the Virgin Mary with unwavering faith. My village of Lourdes was lovely and I would have loved to live there longer before entering the convent.

My monastic life was extremely happy and fulfilling in the heart, despite my illness, because of the prayers and the mystical presence of the Virgin Mary near me. She appeared to me several times when I was at the convent and these apparitions have remained private and personal all my life, at the request of the Virgin Mary. Now, since I have obtained a voice at this moment in history, I hasten to inform you that, indeed, the Virgin Mary had appeared to me after the apparitions of Lourdes when I was at the convent. She was so beautiful and radiant of Light, full of infinite tenderness for me and all humans on earth.

Alleluia! Alleluia! Alleluia! Blessed be the Most Blessed Virgin Mary, the Glory of my life with Christ our Savior. Amen. Alleluia!

Saint *Bernadette* Speaks

11   My children, I am pleased today to be able to speak to you about life in the Great Beyond.

The Virgin Mary, when She had appeared to me in 1858, told me She could not promise that I will be happy in this life, but only in the next. She kept her promise! My life here in Paradise from where I speak now is more enchanting, more magical, more marvelous than I could imagine on earth. I am so happy!

Paradise is extraordinary in its exquisite beauty, in all its pure and vibrant colors, in all its green and perfect nature filled with flowers and plants full of health! The Saints in Paradise and the pure Souls walk around as they wish while praying and glorifying the Lord's graces! The Angels of God are busy with their angelic responsibilities while continually praising the Holy Trinity! Everyone here keeps singing the hymns of praise and joy in gratitude to God our Father Almighty, our Creator to all! Let us give to God—for all His Benefits—very beautiful, very grand, very humble, and very deep Thanksgiving.

Alleluia! Alleluia! Alleluia! Blessed is our God, King of centuries and King of ages, Unique and Invisible, Sovereign Master of the Creation and of all the dimensions known and unknown to men. Amen! Alleluia!

Saint Bernadette Speaks

12   My children, I speak today to you from Paradise near the source of the miraculous Lourdes water.

The Virgin Mary, when She appeared to me in 1858, had affirmed to me the miraculous nature of the water that had sprung from an underground source. My pure heart had believed Her, even without seeing the direct link between the earthly spring and the miraculous spring located in Paradise. You see, faith in the Virgin Mary, in Her Sacred Words, my firm and unwavering belief in Her Divine Words, were sufficient for this beautiful miracle to materialize on earth. Do you see?

The pilgrims who come to the Grotto of Our Lady of Lourdes and who bathe in the miraculous Lourdes water must also have an unwavering faith in the miraculous powers therein. They must believe, without any weakness or inner doubt, in the Virgin Mary, in the miraculous water endowed with supernatural powers and blessed by God, and in me, Saint Bernadette, who intercedes on their behalf before God the Father Almighty.

Faith, therefore, in these three sacred levels of devotion that Divine Providence has provided to the Grotto of Lourdes, that is to say, the abiding and luminous presence of the Virgin Mary, the abiding and luminous presence of

Book 1 | 31

the miraculous water, and my abiding and luminous presence as well as my holy intercession, is necessary for achieving the requested miracles.

God, in all His solicitude and all His Divine Mercy, wishes in the highest degree to grant the miracles requested (for it is He alone Who makes the final decision), but His decision is based on the state of the praying soul.

God knows everything, God hears everything, God sees everything. Be, my children, white as snow, pure as the water of the merciful Lourdes water, and solid in your faith as the walls of the Grotto of the apparitions... and in that, God will be pleased.

Alleluia! Alleluai! Alleluia! Blessed is he who believes without seeing, as this one will obtain mercy. Amen. Alleluia!

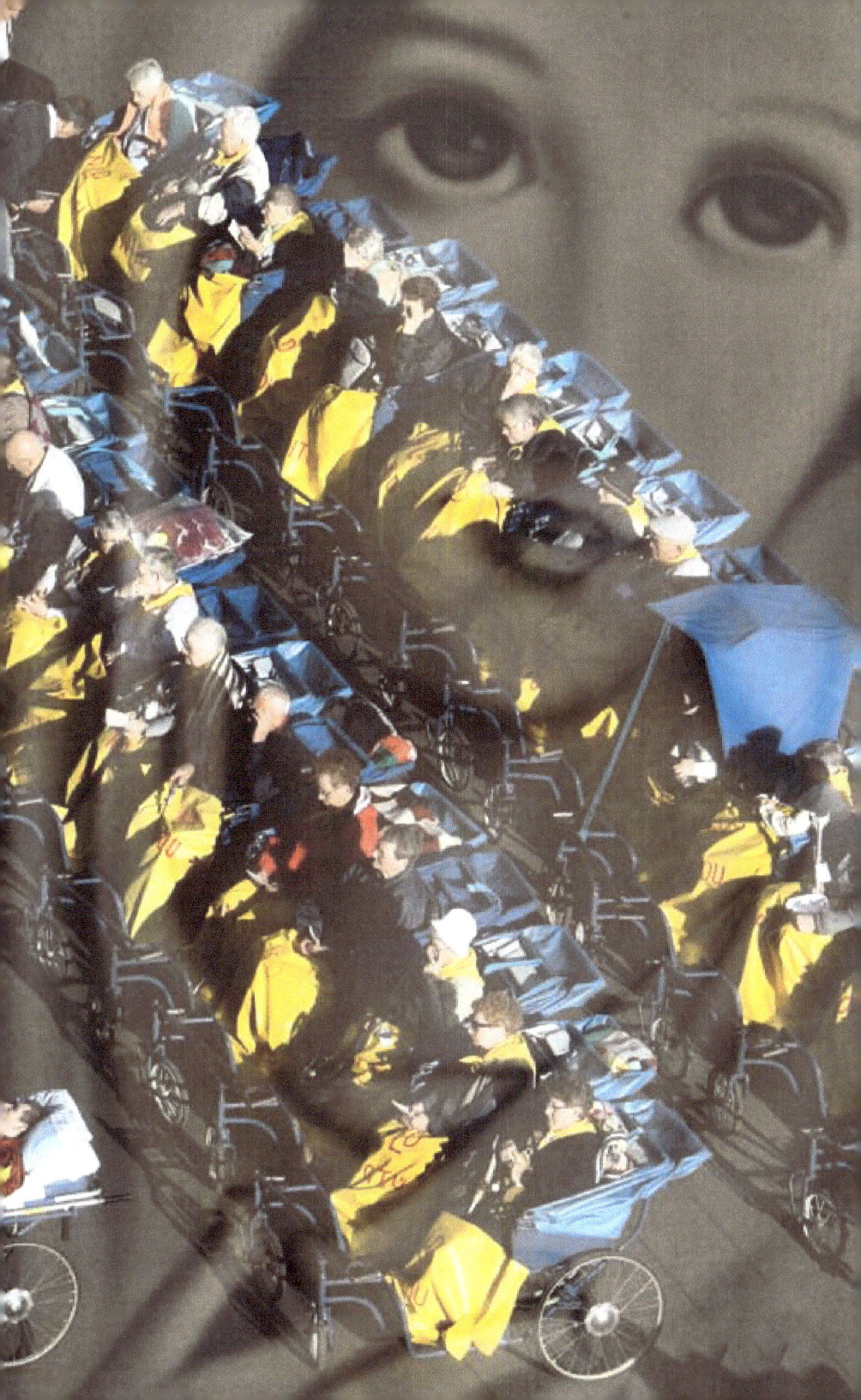

Saint *Bernadette* Speaks

13 My children, my intention today is for you to understand the merits of the miraculous water of the underground fountain of Lourdes.

God, in all His Divine Mercy, decided, on the eve of my encounter with the Virgin Mary in 1858, to offer humanity in distress a physical and tangible instrument in connection with His Supreme Powers over all events taking place on earth, including the healing of the sick.

God is compassion, God is solicitude, God is Divine Mercy, when the soul comes to Him, either directly or through the intercession of the Saints in Paradise. Consequently, when God evaluates a soul to determine its merits, He assesses the depth of a soul's faith in Him.

Alleluia! Alleluia! Alleluia! Blessed is he who believes without seeing, as this one will obtain mercy. Amen. Alleluia!

The miraculous Lourdes water allows the soul to approach God through the intervention of the physical senses involved (contemplating water, drinking water, bathing in water). The soul thirsting for God will be watered immediately, not only by the physical and miraculous water accessible in Lourdes, but especially by Divine Mercy, the long-awaited miracle. Do you see? Meditate today on your connection with God the Father Almighty and imagine a stream of Life and Mercy between you and God.

Alleluia! Alleluia! Alleluia! Blessed is he who sees God in the miraculous Lourdes water, for truly God lives therein. Amen. Alleluia!

Saint Bernadette Speaks

14 My children, give me the joy and the opportunity today to speak to you about my life on earth during the end of my journey.

I became very ill at the end of my life by the decision of God the Father Almighty. Tuberculosis had affected me and had destroyed my bones. The pain was very intense but the Virgin Mary had taught me to offer this pain to God for the conversion of sinners. My faith in Her, my faith in God, my faith in Christ Jesus our Savior, was tremendous and unwavering. That is why the strength to endure the pain was given to me by the grace of the Almighty.

Alleluia! Alleluia! Alleluia! Blessed is he who suffers in the joy of self-offering to God, for suffering in Christ wins the Mercy of God. Amen. Alleluia!

Saint *Bernadette* Speaks

15   My children, I am pleased to be part of your life now. The life that was given to me by God the Father Almighty, when I was Bernadette Soubirous on earth, is not the life I would like you to remember about me. Instead, I wish that you would unite with me in my everyday life in Heaven where I live. For here I am so happy! And my powers have become miraculous thanks to the divine grace granted to me by the Father and for which I am infinitely grateful. Pray! Pray! Pray! And you will be rewarded!

Simply say: "Saint Bernadette, pray for me, before God the Father Almighty, for the obtention of the grace of miracles, by virtue of your gift of miracles and the miraculous Lourdes water, through the bleeding and triumphant Wounds of our Lord Jesus Christ and the Immaculate Heart of Mary. Amen."

I say unto you, I say unto you verily, my powers in Heaven are much greater than you can imagine.

Alleluia! Alleluia! Alleluia! Blessed is he who requests the intercession of Saint Bernadette, the Saint of miracles, for God the Father Almighty in this rejoices greatly. Amen. Alleluia!

Saint *Bernadette* Speaks

16 Dear children, be happy today in the peace of the Lord, for the grace of miracles is granted to you, according to the merits of your heart and your faith in me, Saint Bernadette, a servant of the Virgin Mary, your faith in Her, our Redemptive Mother, your faith in the miraculous Lourdes water which takes its source in Paradise, and above all, your faith in Him, our Creator, the Father Almighty, Ruler of all, in the Name of Christ the Savior.

The grace of miracles is a rare treasure of Divine Providence that is authorized by God the Father Almighty exclusively after His detailed and comprehensive examination of your soul. The grace of miracles allows you, dear child of God, to intercede yourself in order to obtain the Mercy of God Himself with regard to the petition requested.

The grace of miracles is a grace seldom granted by God, for God Himself chooses the soul, and it has to be pure and white as snow, without fear, without attachment to anything on earth, and completely devoted to God in a total and serene abandonment to Him and to His Divine Will.

Blessed are the souls that deserve the grace of miracles, a unique treasure among the treasures in Paradise. Amen. Alleluia!

Saint *Bernadette* Speaks

17   My children, do me the pleasure today to hear you say your rosary!

The daily recitation of the rosary is a powerful and unique weapon against the attacks of the devil. The Most Blessed Virgin Mary, through the universal co-redemptive Powers that were given to Her by God the Father Almighty at the beginning of Creation, can destroy obstacles as well as eliminate the sources of suffering in your life if you ask for Her help.

For the Virgin Mary was conceived at the beginning of Creation, long before the physical mother of Christ Jesus walked on planet earth. Indeed, God the Father Almighty, in all His solicitude and all His Mercy for mankind, has given to us all a Divine Mother, a Mother in Heaven, a Mother of compassion, of consolation, of, liberation, and of extraordinary Powers against the enemy.

Pray my children, pray! Say your Rosary every day, and every day the Blessed Virgin Mary will assist you in all aspects of your life! Amen. Alleluia!

No Light Nor Litany

Must Be Spared

To Honor Thy Grace

Saint Bernadette Speaks

18   My children, I am elated to live in Paradise! And one day, you will also be here with me and the other Saints in Paradise and the Angels of God. Amen! Alleluia!

Let us give glory to God for so much Mercy on your soul, on every soul on earth, and on my sinner's soul before my death in 1879. My pain and agony at the end of my life allowed me to expiate my sins in the Eyes of God and allowed me to enter and cross through the Gates of Paradise.

I was welcomed and celebrated by Christ, my Savior and my God, by the Virgin Mary, my Divine Mother and the Mother of us all in Heaven, by Saint Paul, by the Angels of God including my Guardian Angel, the Holy Spirit, and many other cosmic and universal Forces that you do not know. For the whole Paradise is far greater and far more beautiful than the earth where you live...Oh yes!

Alleluia! Alleluia! Alleluia! Blessed is he who is preparing for Paradise today, for today Paradise is promised him. Amen. Alleluia!

Saint *Bernadette* Speaks

19   My children, I am pleased to get to know you today, regardless of whether or not you are a pilgrim to the Sanctuary of Lourdes. My influence in your life, as well as the influence of the Virgin Mary and the merciful Lourdes water, is independent of your visits to the Grotto of Lourdes. However, it is true that these visits of pilgrimage will increase the magnetic and emotional intensity of our connection and the intensity of your prayers.

   For what is pleasing to God, far beyond a prayer articulated with clarity and precision, is the fervor and the emotion that carry your prayer into the very depths of your heart. Indeed, God the Father Almighty wishes in the highest degree to *feel* your prayers, at the level of your sincerity, your devotion, your faith, your hope, and the intensity of your supplication.

   Pray, then, my dear children, from the very depths of your heart! Very very deeply into your heart! For this is where the Kingdom of God resides! Amen! Alleluia!

Saint *Bernadette* Speaks

20 My children, my friends, my loves, I wish to tell you today how much I love you!

I love you, each and every one of you, when you visit the Sanctuary of Lourdes. I love you, each and every one of you, when you bow down in reverence to Our Lady of Lourdes, the heart open in the hope of the requested miracle. I love you, each and every one of you, when you pray fervently for my divine intercession in order to obtain the much desired miracle. I love you, each and every one of you, when you drink or you sprinkle yourself with the miraculous Lourdes water, with trust and abandonment in the Father's forgiveness. I love you, each and every one of you, when you continue your devotion to the Sanctuary of Lourdes from afar, when you return home, knowing in your heart that the accomplished pilgrimage has changed your life forever.

I love you, each and every one of you, I love you! And I bless you, in the Name of the Father, and of the Son, and of the Holy Spirit. Amen. Alleluia!

Saint *Bernadette* Speaks

21 My children, I am able to perform countless miracles for you, no matter if you visit the Sanctuary of Lourdes or not, by virtue of my grace of miracles, and in the name of Christ Jesus, our Savior and our God, and the Immaculate Heart of Mary.

This grace was given to me by God Himself when I entered Paradise, where the Virgin Mary, Our Lady of Lourdes, was waiting for me with exaltation. Such joy to be in Paradise and to always be alongside our Divine Mother to all! Such release from the world's misery on earth! Such a beautiful gift that is Paradise for the souls who are servants of God! For God will reward every soul who has dedicated his life on earth to the mission that the Father has given him. Glory be to God!

Alleluia! Alleluia! Alleluia! Blessed is he who gives himself body and soul to God on earth, as this one will see Paradise! Amen. Alleluia!

My children, I can now tell you about the great mystery that is Divine Mercy.

Why is it that some pilgrims are healed on many levels and others are not? Divine Mercy is available to all, equally and perfectly. However, the obtention of a miracle of healing stands at a higher level.

Saint *Bernadette* Speaks

22   Divine Mercy can not be qualified or quantified by human evaluation. Be well assured that each and every pilgrim visiting the Sanctuary of Lourdes is a focus of and obtains Divine Mercy. Each pilgrim thus receives spiritual, emotional, psychological, and physical benefits, far more than you can imagine. These results can be manifested clearly, either immediately or later in life; and often the pilgrim does not make the connection between Divine Providence and the visit to Lourdes that goes back many years in the past.

Be well assured that protection, relief, and guidance will be given to you according to your level of faith in the Virgin Mary, our Divine Mother to all, in myself, Bernadette Soubirous, and in the miraculous Lourdes water. We will speak of what is a miracle of healing a little later. For now, let us thank God for all His Blessings.

Alleluia! Alleluia! Alleluia! Blessed be God the Father Almighty, Who is Divine Mercy, destined to all His children. Amen. Alleluia!

Saint *Bernadette* Speaks

23 Nothing is forbidden to me with regard to my involvement in the physical and ethereal planes on earth; I can appear here or there before the soul of my choice. I can also show myself to a soul in many ways: I have the ability to influence dreams, to heal negative emotions, to insert positive ideas, to bring about the solution to this or that problem.

Specifically, according to the Will of God the Father Almighty, I have the ability to perform miracles for you, in the name of our Lord Jesus Christ and the Immaculate Heart of Mary. Such gladness in Paradise when a miracle is granted! Such joy and comfort in the soul and its surrounding family when a miracle is received! For God the Father is Mercy, and I, Saint Bernadette, a servant of God, help you obtain His Mercy by virtue of my gift of miracles.

Alleluia! Alleluia! Alleluia! Blessed be God the Father Almighty, One Sole God Who reigns over all His Creation world without end! Amen. Alleluia!

Saint *Bernadette* Speaks

24 My children, I am pleased with the works accomplished by the servants of God who were called to continue my mission at the Sanctuary of Lourdes. Priests, nuns, deacons, support staff, lay people, are all guided by the Holy Spirit, and sustained by the Love of the Most Blessed Virgin Mary, through Her Son, our Savior, the Lord Jesus Christ, in order to glorify God and His Divine Mercy manifested here at the Sanctuary of Lourdes.

I pray so very hard, dear children, so to allow the works at the service of the great miracle that is the Sanctuary of Lourdes to grow stronger and multiply, now and in the future blessed by God.

Alleluia! Alleluia! Alleluia! Blessed are those who work in Lourdes, for they are servants of God, through the Immaculate Heart of Mary and in the Name of His Wonderful and Luminous Son, our Lord Jesus Christ, our Savior and our God! Amen. Alleluia!

Saint Bernadette Speaks

25 My children, I am able to speak to you today about the underlying nature of miracles.

What is a miracle? A miracle is an act of God that transcends the natural laws governing the three dimensions where you live. This direct intervention of God the Father Almighty in the life of a wandering soul on earth is the result of His Intimate and Personal Decision—called the Divine Will of God the Father Almighty.

The Will of God is unfathomable by anyone, even by us, the inhabitants of Paradise. The Will of God is unchangeable, despite appearances of fluctuations that are observed on earth.

The Will of God is extraordinary in its precision, in its justice, and in its execution. Divine Will is manifested instantly anytime and anywhere, which is why miracles are sudden, rapid, and complete. We will continue the study of the miracle soon.

Alleluia! Alleluia! Alleluia! Blessed be God the Father and blessed be His Divine Will that is allowing you to read these lines blessed by Him. Amen. Alleluia!

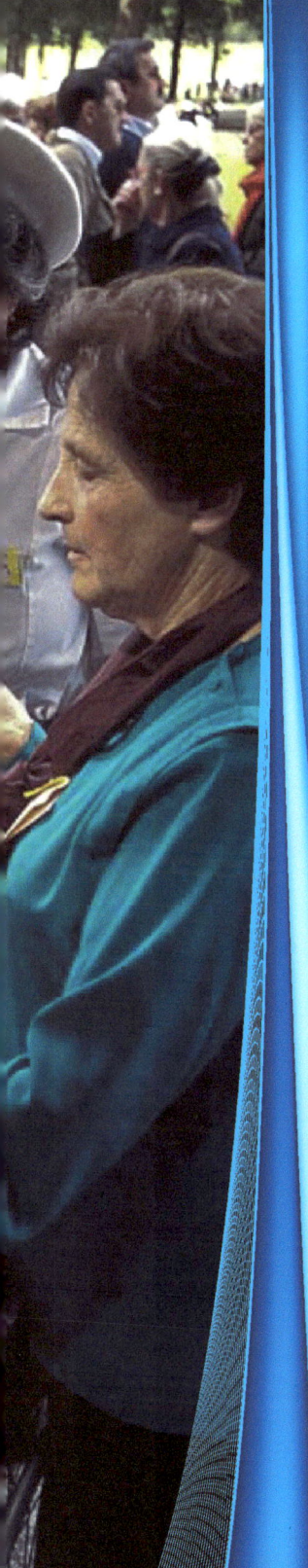

Saint *Bernadette* Speaks

26 My children, let us continue today our study of miracles.

A miracle, as you know, is the result of the divine and exclusive intervention of the Father Almighty, and this miracle touches the life of a soul that He desires to bless. The prayers made by the soul before Him, and the prayers made by the dedicated souls who surround that soul on earth, add up and help pay the debt that this soul owes to God. Moreover, our prayers and intercessions toward this soul—that is to say, those from Paradise, including the Saints in Paradise, the pure Souls, the Angels of God, the Virgin Mary, and Christ Jesus our Savior—are received and honored by God in His Ineffable Heart.

The personal decision that God makes regarding this request represents a cosmic event taking place in all dimensions of the universe, as much in its extraordinary magnitude as in its temporal immediacy. Factors influencing the decision of the Father to grant a miracle cannot be evaluated—or even approached—in any way and by anyone, on earth as in Heaven. The intimate and personal decision of God to grant a miracle is a mystery between the Creator and His Creation. Glory be to God in the Highest Heaven and peace on earth to men of good will!

Alleluia! Alleluia! Alleluia! Blessed be God, God of miracles and God of Mercy! Amen. Alleluia!

Saint Bernadette Speaks

27 My children, I am disappointed to see so little confidence in your clergy.

The priests of your parish and the superiors of the Church make tremendous efforts in order to reach you spiritually, to teach you the Word of God, and to protect you from the assaults of the enemy. Pray! Pray! Pray! Go to church as often as possible! Submit yourself to the Sacrament of Confession as often as possible! Receive Christ in substance in the Sacrament of the Eucharist as often as possible! And read the books of this collection, for these books are blessed by God and are part of His Great Plan of Salvation. For the end times are near and the edification of your soul is fundamental to your salvation in the Eyes of God.

Alleluia! Alleluia! Alleluia! Blessed is he who prays today, for today this one is saved. Amen. Alleluia!

Saint Bernadette Speaks

28 My children, my most dear children, I wish today to speak to you about the Will of God.

The Will of God is ineffable; by this, I wish you to understand that the reasons behind the intimate and personal decisions of God the Father Almighty cannot be shared or disclosed to anyone, on earth as in Heaven.

The decisions of the Father, which constitute His Divine Will on earth as in Heaven, are executed and manifested immediately, without delay, on all planes of the universe known and unknown to men.

The Divine Will of God applies to all His Creation, at any time and anywhere, through all the Kingdoms belonging to Him, including the animal kingdom, the plant kingdom, the mineral kingdom, humanity, the Kingdom of Heaven, and other worlds that you do not know.

Saint Bernadette Speaks

The secret of happiness and peace on earth is to accept and to conform at any time to the Will of God, whatever it may be, as it manifests in your life, second by second, minute by minute, hour by hour.

God knows you perfectly, God loves you so infinitely, God leads you entirely, each and everyone of you. The passage of an inner doubt with respect to the supremacy of God in your life generates an opposition to His Will at the mental or emotional level, resulting in elements of anxiety, fear, sadness, or anger infiltrating your life. Any event that is an apparent injustice committed against you is a mistake of human understanding.

Pray! Pray! Pray! Ask for clarification and solution to the problems you meet and you will be answered! Amen. Alleluia!

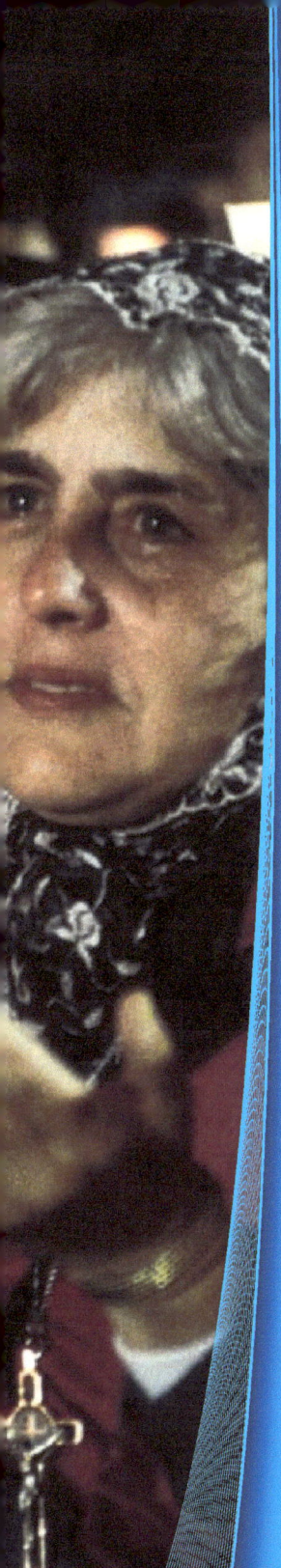

Saint Bernadette Speaks

29 My children, I am honored to teach you the fundamentals of the miracle, for the miracle will from now on be part of your heart.

Indeed, the grace of miracles, which is a wonderful and dramatic grace of God, is given to you today according to the merits of your heart and your degree of faith in us—that is to say, the Most Blessed Virgin Mary, Our Lady of Lourdes, the miraculous Lourdes water, and myself, Saint Bernadette Soubirous, a servant of God.

Pray, my children, pray! Pray that God the Father Almighty confers on you the grace of miracles! For God the Father Almighty delights in blessing the souls who seek His Blessing and the obtention of the divine graces that only He attributes.

Alleluia! Alleluia! Alleluia! Blessed are the souls who pray to obtain the grace of miracles, for God the Father Almighty in this rejoices. Amen. Alleluia!

Alleluia! Alleluia! Alleluia! Blessed is he who prays today, for today this one is saved. Amen. Alleluia!

Saint *Bernadette* Speaks

30 My children, the time has come to speak to you about my role in Heaven.

Here in Heaven, in the Kingdom of God conceived by God, I am in charge of all the miracles and other benefits that are related to the Grotto at Lourdes where the Most Blessed Virgin Mary appeared to me.

This beautiful miracle of modern times has been allowed through the intense prayers of the Most Blessed Virgin Mary, in order to increase faith in Her, and in order to glorify God the Father Almighty.

I was chosen, I, Saint Bernadette Soubirous, for divine and cosmic reasons that belong only to God. Suffice it to say that this beautiful miracle took place in 1858 by virtue of the Powers and the Love of the Most Blessed Virgin Mary, our Heavenly Mother to all...

Alleluia! Alleluia! Alleluia! Blessed be the Most Blessed Virgin Mary, Mother of God and Mother of men. Amen. Alleluia!

Saint Bernadette Speaks

31 My children, I am here with you when I speak to you and I will be with you until the end of times—and beyond.

This beautiful miracle that is my presence at your side, here, now and forever, is the result of the mercy contained in the five crosses that were earned by the Logos of Saint Paul. I am infinitely grateful to God the Father Almighty Who is granting you His Divine Mercy at this time of your life through this book blessed by Him. I am also grateful to Marie-Josée, the one who is taking this dictation at this time. Marie-Josée is the essence of Saint Paul on earth and she is pursuing her mission with zeal, faith, and determination. Without her, this book would not have reached you.

Alleluia! Alleluia! Alleluia! Blessed be God the Father Almighty for so much mercy poured forth on your soul today! Amen. Alleluia!

Saint Bernadette Speaks

32 My children, I am there with you, at this time when you are reading these lines, and I will be with you until the end of times—and beyond.

The Divine Mercy granted to the readers of this book, as well as all the other books in this collection, is the result of the magnificent work achieved by the lineage of the five crosses. The five crosses symbolize the Logos of Saint Paul the Apostle and contain an Infinite and Unique Mercy ordained according to the Decision of the Father.

I thank Marie-Josée here again, the essence of Saint Paul on earth, the one taking this dictation at this time, and who is accomplishing her duties to perfection, in order to allow the salvation of your soul as determined by the Decision of God.

Alleluia! Alleluia! Alleluia! Blessed be the five crosses of the Legion of Saint Paul, symbol of Eternal Life offered by God! Amen. Alleluia!

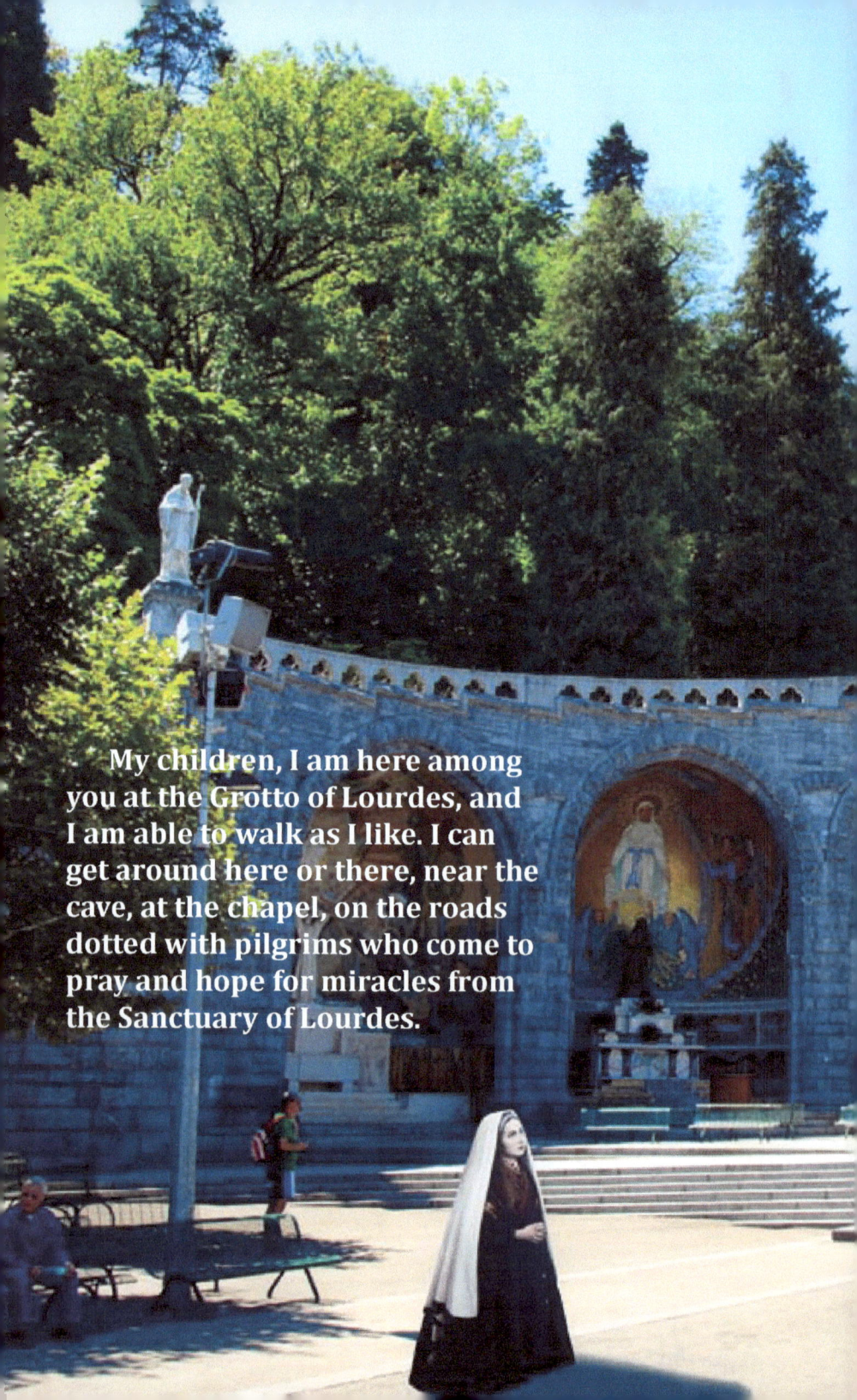

My children, I am here among you at the Grotto of Lourdes, and I am able to walk as I like. I can get around here or there, near the cave, at the chapel, on the roads dotted with pilgrims who come to pray and hope for miracles from the Sanctuary of Lourdes.

Saint *Bernadette* Speaks

33 Such joy in my Divine Heart when I see hearts open and filled with faith and hope! Such sadness when I see instead of hearts hardened and closed, disillusioned by the disappointments of life and filled with sadness and bitterness!

Pray, my children, pray! Come visit me here at the Sanctuary and know that I am there, among you, as well as here inside your heart, and in the same supernatural way, nice and warm in Paradise. Know that I hear all your prayers, whispered in the depths of your heart or spoken aloud, each and everyone of you, and that I carry them all before the Father Almighty, through the Immaculate Heart of the Virgin Mary, Our Lady of Lourdes, and in the Holy Name of Jesus. Pray, pray, pray! And you will be answered!

Alleluia! Alleluia! Alleluia! Blessed is he who has faith in me, Saint Bernadette, in the Most Blessed Virgin Mary, Our Lady of Lourdes, in Her Son, our Wonderful Savior, our Lord Jesus Christ and in our Father Almighty, for this one will be rewarded. Amen. Alleluia!

Saint Bernadette Speaks

34 My children, today I hasten to tell you about my childhood. I was born into a poor family, as you know, but my family was very religious and loving.

My mother, already distressed by the financial difficulties of our family, was overwhelmed and confused before the surreal events that God had ordained for me. Fortunately, the Holy Spirit permitted the accelerated understanding of the mysteries of the apparitions of the Virgin Mary before me, so my mission went on according to Divine Will.

Alleluia! Alleluia! Alleluia! Blessed be my mother on earth and my Mother in Heaven! Amen. Alleluia!

Saint Bernadette Speaks

35   My children, I approach the end of my presentation originating from Heaven and originating from the Grotto of Lourdes.

Your life will never be the same, my beloved, my child, despite the appearances of your living environment. For your soul is now in my hands, dear beautiful little soul, and I undertake to make your life miraculous as of today.

I will speak to you again very soon.

Do me the favor, my child, to say your rosary every day with me, Saint Bernadette, born Bernadette Soubirous, and with the Most Blessed Virgin Mary, Our Lady of Lourdes.

I love you.

I bless you in the Name of the Father, and of the Son, and of the Holy Spirit. Amen.

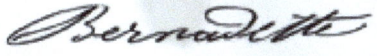

Afterword

You have now entered the world of Saint Bernadette, a charismatic and powerful Saint who always works fervently in collaboration with Our Lady of Lourdes, Jesus our Lord, and other Saints in Heaven to present your wishes and petitions before God the Father Almighty. Whether or not you have been to Lourdes or are planning to go on a pilgrimage there, Bernadette will give you her undivided attention and eternal love.

Pray often to Saint Bernadette and request her mighty intercession without hesitation. You will be enchanted with granted petitions that will start to materialize very quickly! Trust in Bernadette; call upon her name often through the beautiful Heart of Our Lady of Lourdes and the Sacred Heart of Jesus. Amen! Alleluia!

Marie-Josée

About the Author

Marie-Josée Thibault's life is in no way similar to yours. When she wakes, the saints of Heaven visit her, talk to her, teach her, and pray intensely with her. When such mystical sessions draw to a close, she greets with great respect and deep reverence the Masters of the Heavenly Court. This servant of the Lord spends the rest of the day in the company of her guardian angel, who continues her spiritual education and ceaselessly protects her from the perils of this fallen world.

Bestowed by the Heavenly Father, her gifts of clairvoyance and clairaudience allow her to remain in continuous contact with the supernatural dimension juxtaposed with ours, where the soul is born of the Spirit through Jesus and Mary. She prays that, one day soon, the entire human race will give glory to the Father, the Son, and the Holy Spirit.

Also by Author

Saint Padre Pio Speaks: Book 1

Abba, Your Father, Speaks: Book I

Abba, Your Father, Speaks: Book II

Angel Gabriel Speaks: Book 1

Saint Beethoven Speaks Book 1

Dear Humanity: Book 1

Dear Humanity: Book 2

Saint Therese of Lisieux

FREE DOWNLOAD

Get your free copy of :
"Saint Padre Pio Speaks: Book 1"
when you sign up to the author's VIP mailing list!
Get started here:

www.abbamyfatheriloveyou.com

www.ingramcontent.com/pod-product-compliance
Lightning Source LLC
Chambersburg PA
CBHW041626220426
43663CB00001B/25